The Lord redeems his servants; no one will be condemned who takes refuge in him. Psalm 34:22

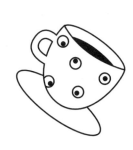

But when the time had fully come, God sent his Son, born of a woman, born under law, to redeem those under law, that we might receive the full rights of sons. Galatians 4:4

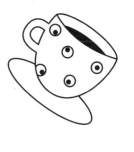

Fear not, for I have redeemed you; I have summoned you by name; you are mine. Isaiah 43:1

Put your hope in the LORD, for with him is unfailing love and full redemption. Psalm 130:7

In him we have redemption through his blood, the forgiveness of sins,

in accordance with
the riches of
God's grace.
Ephesians 1:7

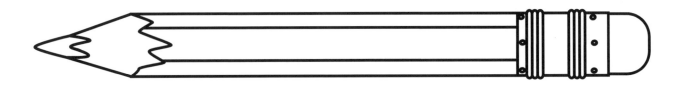

He has rescued us from the dominion of darkness and brought us into the kingdom

of the Son he loves,
in whom we have
redemption, the
forgiveness of sins.
Colossians 1:13-15

I know that my Redeemer lives, and that in the end he will stand upon the earth. Job 19:25

He redeemed my soul from going down to the pit, and I will live to enjoy the light. Job 33:28

Into your hands I commit my spirit; redeem me, O LORD, the God of truth. Psalm 31:5

You were bought at a price; do not become slaves of men.

1 Corinthians 7:23

Christ redeemed us from the curse of the law of the law

by becoming a curse for us,

for it is written: "Cursed is everyone who is hung on a tree." Galatians 3:13

If you lost something and the only way you could get it returned was to pay some money for it - then you would pay the money. That is redeeming something - it means buying it back. Jesus Christ redeemed his people at a costly price. Sin separates sinners from God and the only way for Jesus to bring his people back to God was for Jesus to take the punishment that they deserved. Jesus took all of God's anger against sin when he died on the cross. This is what redemption is: Jesus gave his life in exchange for ours. He became sin so that we could be holy.